THE LAW OF ACTION

ROLAND BYRD

THE LAW OF ACTION

HOW TO HIT YOUR TARGET EVERY TIME

Publications

This book is available at special quantity discounts for bulk purchase for sales promotions, premiums, fund-raising, and educational needs. For details email Roland@RolandByrd.com.

Published by: CYL Publications: http://cylp.co

ISBN: 1-940324-12-2
ISBN-13: 978-1-940324-12-8

Contents

Introduction

I want you to reach your goals, to witness your dreams come to life. I want you to feel the fires of creation burning like a bonfire within your heart, screaming for release. I want you to feel the joy of creation and the satisfaction of staying the course. I want to hear your success stories, to know that you're giving life your all, that you're creating amazing results, and that you're making the world a better place!

Why?

First, because *you deserve to reach your goals.*

Second, because I know what it's like to miss your goals. I know how frustrating it is to work long and hard and still fall short. I know what it's like to absolutely know you can do something but be unable to figure out what you're missing, why you aren't getting there. I've done it often enough over the years.

Then I discovered the missing piece. And through that discovery I intuitively understood how all the parts fit. Before I felt like I'd been working on a giant jig-saw puzzle that was missing key pieces. Then after my discovery I found the missing pieces right under my nose and the puzzle came together easily.

Understand, I was great at taking action on my dreams and goals. I've taken consistent action on a daily basis for nearly eight years as I write this. I've made amazing changes in my life, completely redesigned myself as a person, and accomplished epic things. But for some reason I was still hit and miss on my big goals. I was hot, then cold. I'd produce magnificent results for a time and then stall, like a car spinning its wheels on ice.

I had goals. I wrote them down. I made them specific. I took consistent action. But something was missing. I didn't have all the parts necessary to consistently hit my goals.

Perhaps that sounds, looks, or feels familiar?

Then it hit me. The Ah-Ha moment. I never had a real plan! That was my missing piece. Yours might be different. But The Law of Action isn't simply a book about creating a plan. It's much, much more. The Law of Action dives deeply into all of the critical parts necessary for you to reach or exceed any realistic goal you set. Now, I only say realistic because if your goal is to survive in outer-space without a space-suit on... Well, this book won't really help you there.

As long as you're willing to follow all of the steps in The Law of Action, as long as you're willing to put in the time and effort, you're going to reach more goals than ever before. And I promise, You'll be thrilled at your new results.

How can I say that with such confidence?

Once I realized what I was doing wrong, I immediately used all of the processes in this book to write, edit, and publish the book! I'm using the processes in The Law of Action for all of my goals now and they're coming true faster than ever before.

So *Read The Law of Action,* Put the processes to the test, and let me know how well it's working for you.

Roland Byrd
10/19/2016

The Law of Action

Nothing Happens Without Action

Everything you do, everything you have, everything in your life—good or bad subjectively—is the result of an action. Some of these actions were yours. Some were the actions of others. Some are actions of Nature—storms, floods, earthquakes, plants blooming, sunshine, wind, rain, etc. Some are even actions of biology.

All of these actions have one thing in common. They produced results. These results, combined with your opinion of the results *and the actions you took based on your opinions*, equal the current state of your life.

That means; regardless of what's happened in your life, regardless of whether you liked or didn't like something, regardless of whether you were hurt, not hurt, happy, or sad, *you always chose your response.* You might not have realized it at the time...

But you did.

You chose what things meant. And then you acted on your choices, on the meaning you assigned each event.

You can only take actions that fit the meaning you give something. You're the only one who gets to choose what something means to you.

You.

Your Interpretations. Your Choices. Your Actions. Your Results.

That puts accountability for your life right on your shoulders. You might not like that. You might feel that's unfair.

If you truly want to succeed, you'll get over it.

When I first discovered that the state of my life—screwed up mess that it was—was my responsibility, I felt the weight of my life settle squarely on my shoulders, grinding me into the ground.

"That's not fair!" I screamed inside. I wanted to rage against God, "How can it be my fault? How can this possibly be My Fault?"

I couldn't blame my parents.

I couldn't blame society.

I couldn't blame my childhood.

I couldn't blame any external force.

It was all on me. Talk about a painful realization.

But then I experienced one of the most profound awakenings of my life: If everything in my life was the result of my actions, then that also meant I could *change* my *actions* and *change* my *life!*

In an instant I was transformed from the victim of my history to the champion of my future. I finally understood that I have the power to create my future. I have the power to choose my life's path, to achieve anything I desire.

You have this power too. *We all do.*

Few use it *but all have it.*

So what are actions?

They're more than physical. Every thought you entertain is an action. Every time you make a choice, that's an action. Everything you do is an action. Everything you choose not to do is also an action. Every time you interpret events and the things you do because of your interpretations *are all actions!*

The *Law of Action* impacts all areas of your life because your actions create your life.

The trick is choosing the right actions to shape your life as you desire.

The *Law of Action* is simple.

Nothing Happens Without Action.

The secret is using the *Law of Action* effectively. That's what this book is about, how to use the *Law of Action* to create the life you desire.

Ready to discover how to use the *Law of Action* to make your goals and dreams reality?

Great!

Keep reading...

The Missing Link

"Yesterday I was clever, so I wanted to change the world. Today I am wise, so I am changing myself."
— *Rumi*

You've got your goals and dreams. You keep them in mind and focus on them regularly. You've even written them down. You imagine what your life is like when you've achieved your goals. And you reach some of them. But something's missing. Your results are inconsistent. Somehow you seem to miss the big goals, the ones that really matter.

I know; it's frustrating. I've been there.

So what is it? Why aren't you reaching all your goals? What's the missing link?

You need a bridge between your current life and the life you'll have when you reach your major goals. Three things create that bridge; a plan, action, and feedback.

Think of your goals like a sailboat. To successfully sail to their destination, the sailboat captain needs wind, a rudder, a navigation system (compass, GPS, sextant, maps, etc.), and to know where they're going. That's a simplified explanation but you get the idea.

Having a Goal means you know your destination. Goals without a plan are like a sailboat with no rudder, you may know your destination, but you'll have a difficult time setting or correcting course. Goals without action are like a sailboat without wind, they're not going very far. Goals without a feedback mechanism—a way for you to pay attention and track the results you're getting—are like a sailboat with no navigation system, there's no way to tell if you're going the right way.

As you understand, all four parts are critical to reaching your goals. You must have a goal, a plan, take action, *and* monitor your results so you can correct your approach as needed.

Without all four parts, you'll struggle reaching major goals. You might drift a little, you might even make sporadic progress, but you won't consistently *move toward and reach your goals.*

Smaller goals are easier to reach. It's like crossing a small pond. You can see the other shore. So you can usually fumble your way across. Heck, you can paddle with your hands if needed. That's why *you're good at reaching* your smaller *goals.* You've got desire and you're willing to do something about it, so you'll eventually make it across.

Larger, long term goals are like crossing one of the Great Lakes or the ocean. You can't see the other side. So you'd better have wind, navigation, a rudder, and k*now your destination!*

Most goals setters are good at one, maybe two parts of effective goal reaching. Some are good at three of the four. But the masters, the people who seem to always reach their goals, those are the ones who *consistently practice all four steps.*

This is where *The Law of Action* come into play.

All four parts of successful goal realization *require action.* You must take action to write your goals. You must take action to create your plan. You must take action on your plan. And you must take action to heed the feedback you're getting and correct course as needed.

Without action all you've got are hopes, wishes, and dreams. There's nothing wrong with hopes, wishes, and dreams. Just understand that in that state they're only ideas and rarely reach fulfillment.

Remember, the *Law of Action* states:

Nothing Happens Without Action

That means: *You Must Take Action to Realize Your Dreams!*

It's time to unleash the Law of Action in your life!

Next we'll dive into why you aren't getting what you want.

Action Points:

- To reach major goals, you need a bridge between the current state of your life and the way your life will be when you achieve those goals.
- A plan, action, and feedback create that bridge.
- The four parts to effective goal achievement are:
  - Having a goal
  - Having a plan
  - Taking Action
  - Using a feedback mechanism

Why You Aren't Getting What You Want

"It is an awesome thing to comprehend that what a human being dreams and imagines can be realized."
— Vanna Bonta

You understand the reason you're not reaching all of your goals is because you're missing one of the four critical parts to effective goal fulfillment. Here they are again:

- You must have a goal
- You must create a plan
- You must take action on your plan
- You must monitor your results and adjust as needed

Perhaps the thought, *"I know that already,"* crossed your mind. If that's the case then please *pay even more attention.* As T. Harv Eker—Bestselling author and Multi-Millionaire—teaches, when your brain says *"I know that"* it's discounting the information as unimportant. When that happens you simply need say, "*Thank you*", to your mind and then *pay even more attention.*

Why?

Your subconscious mind doesn't like change. It likes the patterns you've developed over your life and resists when you're creating new ones. Thoughts like, "I know that already", are your subconscious mind trying to make you stay in your old patterns.

But here's the rub, your old patterns weren't consistently getting you what you want.

To get what you want you must change your patterns.

"How do I *change my patterns?*"

I'm glad you asked!

One of the first steps in changing old patterns is to recognize them. Thoughts that run counter to your new goals are red flags, signs that your subconscious mind is resisting.

When those thoughts enter your mind you simply say _____ _____.

Right, you simply say, "*Thank you*" to your mind and then continue what you were doing.

Got it?

Great!

Let's examine each of the four parts to effective goal reaching in more detail. We'll look at them from all sides and listen to what they're telling us.

You *Must* Have a Goal

This seems self-explanatory... but you might be surprised how many people fail to do this one simple step. Your goal is your destination. If you don't know your destination you'll never reach it. If you only vaguely know your destination, you might get in the general vicinity but you won't hit your target. That means you'll fail to get the results you want. But when you know your exact destination, *that's when your goal takes on true power!*

We'll cover goal setting in detail later. For now just remember that having a goal is critical to your success.

You *Must* Create a Plan

This is one where people consistently fall short. Lots of us are good at creating our goals; great goals with lots of detail, true vision, and positive emotion behind them. But then we either have no plan or only an idea of how we'll achieve the goal with no defined steps.

Does that work?

It never worked for me or anyone else that I know, not on big goals. If you've never created a plan for achieving your goals, when you examine the results you're getting you'll discover it never worked for you either.

Remember; creating a plan is as important as having a goal. We'll cover planning in detail later.

You *Must* Take Action on Your Plan

Action is the fire burning beneath the hot-air balloon of your goal. If there's no fire, the balloon is just an empty sack on the ground. Sure it's colorful and has potential, amazing potential, but until you add that fire it's not going anywhere.

Like the hot-air balloon, when you start the fire beneath your goal it takes a while to fill it and get it off the ground. But once you're in the air it takes smaller burns to stay in the sky than it did to lift off. Once you're taking consistent action on your goal you build momentum. *Momentum creates miracles!* Remember that.

You *Must* Monitor Your Results and Adjust as Needed

You understand it's critical to take action on your goals. You'll get farther by taking action than you ever will by wishing. But if you fail to monitor your results, you'll have a hard time knowing if the action you're taking is effective.

Dr. Stephen Covey uses an analogy in his *7 Habits of Highly Effective People* that's spot on. It doesn't matter how hard you're hacking away at the undergrowth, blazing a trail through the jungle... You can make great progress, but if you're in the wrong jungle you'll never reach your destination.

That's why paying attention to the results you're getting is so important. When you take action on your goal things start happening. It's up to you to determine if those things are carrying you closer to your goal or farther away.

Even actions that bring you closer to your goal must be monitored. That's how you fine tune them and either reach your goal faster or surpass it.

You recognize now that you haven't been getting what you want because you haven't been using all four steps necessary to successfully achieve your goals. That means you're also accepting accountability for your success or failure in these areas.

This is a great time to define failure. Failure only means you didn't get the results you wanted or expected. When things don't work out many people feel that they're a failure. That's a sad place to live. I know; I used to live there. When you fail it means there's more you need to learn or do so *you* can *succeed*.

The only true failure is when you give up.
— Roland Byrd

In reality, failure is simply a teacher. It tells you what you're doing wrong and helps you learn what to do differently. When you use it that way, it helps you grow. Without failure and feedback, you'd never master anything. When something doesn't work the way you expected or hoped, it's best to do three things.

1. Pay attention to what worked! There's no need to discard the parts that were successful just because the whole thing didn't work out.

2. Examine your results and discover what you need to change. Then create a new plan that includes your changes.

3. The next time you try, use your modified plan!

Now keep repeating steps 1 – 3 until you succeed!

Over the next few chapters we'll cover each the four steps in detail. We'll identify possible pitfalls, reveal ways you'll avoid them, and go over steps *you* can *take now* to start effectively implementing each of the four steps. By the time you're done with this book you'll have all the tools you need to create *and* achieve effective goals and you'll be well on your way to mastering the *Law of Action!*

Next we'll reveal the truth about your subconscious mind and how to make it your ally.

Action Points:
*   You Must Create a Goal
*   You Must Create a Plan
*   You Must Take Action on Your Plan
*   You Must Monitor Your Results and Adjust Your Actions Accordingly

Your Subconscious Mind

"Faith is to believe what you do not see; the reward of this faith is to see what you believe."
— Saint Augustine

Until recently the Subconscious Mind was overlooked by many on their quest for a fulfilled life. It was ignored because like the base of an iceberg it's out of sight. Most people live with an "out of sight, out of mind" attitude. But ignoring your subconscious mind is a recipe for disaster. It's a guaranteed way to miss your goals.

The truth is our subconscious minds and subconscious beliefs are the biggest factors when it comes to our habits and behavioral patterns. Unless you turn your subconscious into your ally it will continually undermine your efforts because it wants things to stay the same. It likes the status-quo.

But there's hope because with a little effort you can and will discover how to reprogram your subconscious mind so it becomes your ally.

Here's an excerpt from my first book, *Your Blue print, Life by Design* that sheds light on your subconscious mind's inner workings.

Subconscious Beliefs

Did you know your Subconscious Beliefs are largely responsible for the results you get in life?

It's True!

These beliefs are *Your Blueprint.* Think of them as the autopilot that engages when you aren't consciously controlling your life—which is most of the time. Better yet, imagine a burly co-pilot who insists on flying a different direction than you want. You can fight and fight your co-pilot, but he's a lot stronger than you (80% to 90% stronger) and in the end you'll lose the battle.

Right now you might think, "Great! So I'm not in control of my life! It's my subconscious that's running the show..."

Pause for a moment because there's great news! You can *reprogram Your Blueprint!*

Where force fails, you can talk sense into your subconscious mind. Realize that your subconscious doesn't necessarily listen to reason; it deals with feelings and beliefs. But once you learn to speak its language *You'll convince it that what you want is best.* Then your subconscious mind will put all its considerable power and energy into getting you where you want to go. That means the burly co-pilot will change course and fly toward the destination of your dreams instead of the destination he originally wanted.

Cast aside your old beliefs and behavioral patterns that came from living life as the victim of your history. *Program your subconscious mind with new, empowering beliefs and behavioral patterns.* Start becoming the person you always knew you could be! Start creating the life you desire!

Once your subconscious understands that what you want and what it wants are the same, you'll fly to heights of joy, happiness, and success you've only imagined before!

Rewrite Your Blueprint and in a short time you'll realize the results you're getting from life are aligning with your goals and dreams!

Why?

For the first time in your life your subconscious mind is working for you because your subconscious beliefs align with your desires!

Become one of the heroes of your life.

The greatest thing about being human is the ability to take charge of our lives. Accept accountability today. Realize that, though your subconscious beliefs steer your life, *you control those beliefs.*

So... "Just how do I reprogram my subconscious mind?"

Great question!

There are many methods you can use to alter your subconscious beliefs. Among the most popular are:

- Affirmations
- Hypnotherapy
- Self-Hypnosis
- Subliminal Recordings

Let's quickly examine benefits of each method.

Affirmations

Affirmations can easily be used any time and any place. Just repeat them out loud, under your breath, or say them in your mind and smile. If you make them catchy you'll find yourself repeating them often. That's a good thing. The more you repeat them the stronger they become.

The secret to good affirmations is to combine powerful positive emotions with a simple phrase that embodies the successful achievement of your goal. When you add strong emotion to something, your subconscious automatically marks it as important. The repetition of your affirmation, combined with intense emotions, works double-time at shifting your subconscious beliefs.

Here's an example:

If your goal is to get rid of unwanted body fat, you could use one of these affirmations:

- More and more I make healthy food choices!
- Every day I get stronger and leaner!
- I love feeling healthy and fit!

Notice these are phrased in positive ways and they focus on the process of improving. This reduces the friction created when you tell your subconscious something that isn't either obviously true or that you don't believe yet.

Think about it. No matter what your fitness or health level, you can easily make healthier food choices, you can start exercising. You can get stronger and leaner every day. You can love the feeling of being healthy and fit.

All these things are true. Zero resistance.

Perhaps you're wondering, "How do I create strong positive emotions around my affirmation?"

I'm glad you asked.

In this example; imagine how good it feels when you're healthy and fit. Your body feels amazing, it moves easily. You have greater energy and stamina. You can do more without tiring. Activities that were out of reach are easy for you now. Feel how grateful you are for your new lifestyle. Feel these things as if they were *reality now* and then hold those feelings as you repeat your affirmations.

The combination of powerful emotions *and* consistent repetition of your affirmations is like a lightning strike sending these messages deep into your subconscious.

Affirmations work by creating new pathways in your subconscious mind. The stronger the new pathway becomes, the stronger your subconscious mind's desire to create your new reality.

Repeat your chosen affirmation over and over. Every time you think of it, say your affirmation 5 to 10 times. At first you're telling your subconscious that something is true in a way that reduces its resistance to the new belief. Since your subconscious can't tell the difference between imagination and reality, in time it believes it. After that you're reminding your subconscious how important this new belief is, which helps shift it from a transient belief to a permanent one.

As soon as your subconscious mind adopts your new belief, it starts searching for ways to make it reality!

Using our fitness example; that means you'll start feeling motivated to do things like change your diet, exercise regularly, and drink plenty of water! It's like your subconscious mind becomes your training partner. All because *you shifted your subconscious beliefs.*

A favorite method of mine, and something I highly recommend, is to record your affirmations, save the audio on your phone—you can also use an iPod or MP3 player—and then listed to your affirmations on a loop throughout the day. This fills your subconscious mind with positive messages while you're otherwise engaged. In essence, your affirmations become positive background noise for your day.

This powerful technique sends your affirmations directly into your subconscious mind because your conscious mind is busy with other tasks.

I often have a single earbud in—with my affirmations playing softly in the background. That way I can hear others, know what's going on around me, and still fill my subconscious with positive messages of my choosing!

The trick is consistency. Zig Ziglar often said his research proved that listening to an audio sixteen times plants it firmly in your subconscious mind. I've personally confirmed this. I strongly recommend listening to your affirmations for sixteen days initially and then once a week after that as a tune-up.

Give it a try. *You'll be amazed* at your results

To help you create powerful affirmations, which will assist you in the fulfillment of your goals, I've created an affirmation starter kit for you!

Download it here: http://bit.ly/AffirmationKit

Hypnotherapy

Hypnotherapy works by first placing you in a deeply relaxed state, like a waking dream. In that state your conscious mind is quieted and your subconscious mind becomes highly receptive. This powerful state allows messages to go directly into your subconscious.

Like affirmations, hypnotherapy is most effective with repetition. I've had great success with this method and highly recommend it.

You can go to a licensed hypnotherapist and have them work with you directly. You can also *buy hypnotic recordings* that target areas you're working on and listen to them as you fall asleep at night.

Since hypnotherapy speaks directly to your subconscious, choose a hypnotherapist you can trust and that you feel good about. *Trust your intuition.*

I personally recommend hypnotic recordings by Dr. Steve G. Jones. He is a leader in his field and has hundreds of recordings to choose from.

Visit this link and start leveraging the power of hypnotherapy today!:

http://bit.ly/HypnosisSteveGJones

Self-Hypnosis

Self-Hypnosis can be as effective as hypnotherapy. The difference is that you're hypnotizing yourself and then delivering the messages to your own subconscious.

Self-hypnosis is a great tool because it's infinitely customizable. Anything you want to work on you can, immediately.

I've used this two ways, both with great success. The first is the traditional way. I choose a message, hypnotized myself, and then deliver the message. The second is a modified method. I create my own hypnotic recording that walks me through the hypnosis and then delivers the message.

The only drawback to the first method is that you might fall asleep before you deliver your message.

The power in the second method is that you're delivering the message in your own voice. That means you're hearing the message in a voice that you trust and instantly relate to. It takes more setup because you must first choose your message, then script it, and record it. But it's worth the effort.

Here's a story from my life that shows the power of self-hypnosis:

Jobless

I was out of work. Less than a year previously I was earning nearly 100K a year. But then I'd lost that job—through my own actions. Since that time I'd tried a few entrepreneurial ventures with little luck and less income. I was on unemployment but that was only a small fraction of what I used to earn. I wasn't supporting my family. The bills were piling up. My family was living in poverty. And I wasn't sure what to do.

I needed to find work, *fast*.

On a feeling, I went to the local book store and wandered the isles. Then my eyes were drawn to a book on self-hypnosis. I picked it up. It was an older book. So old that it came with a companion cassette tape. But it felt right. It was $10.00. That was a lot to me then, but I bought it anyway and took it home. Then I found an old Walkman, and listened to the tape.

The recording was a training session in self-hypnosis. It walked me through exactly how to hypnotize myself and then installed trigger words—so I could enter the hypnotic state quickly in the future. I listened to it every day for a week. Once I felt comfortable with the technique I gave it a go, focusing on finding work.

As soon as I was done with my self-hypnosis session I felt prompted to get in my car and start looking for work. So I grabbed a stack of my resumes and drove around. I had no idea where I was supposed to go. But I paid close attention to my feelings while I searched. When I felt an internal nudge to turn up a street I would. When I saw a business and felt I should approach, I parked, walked in, handed them my resume, and explained that I was willing and eager to work.

After an hour or so, I turned up a narrow street with battered buildings on one side and old shops on the other. It didn't look promising *but it felt right.*

I trusted my feelings. I looked around. My eyes were drawn to a boat yard, for storage and maintenance. I'd never worked on a boat in my life. But I stopped there and talked to the owner.

He wasn't hiring but he had a friend who might be. He called his friend and I was hired on the spot. Starting the next morning I was on a crew that shrink-wrapped boats to protect them from heavy snow and the elements during the winter.

I'd never done it before. Until that day I didn't even know shrink-wrapping boats was a job!

But they admired my desire to find work and my willingness to look for it door-to-door. So they hired me.

It wasn't a great paying job. Only $10.00 an hour. But *it was a start.* I was back in the work force and determined to never be unemployed again!

All because I tried self-hypnosis, listened to the inspiration I received, and Took Action!

Subliminal Recordings

Subliminal Recordings have gained popularity lately. I've been using them for years with great success. They work by combining positive affirmations with relaxing music. The affirmations are barely audible and your conscious mind ignores them. But your subconscious mind is always listening. It takes in the messages while you're doing other things.

Just like affirmations, hypnotherapy, and self-hypnosis, subliminal recordings send messages directly to your subconscious mind. When listened to repeatedly, these messages form new, empowering subconscious beliefs.

That's what you want!

I first learned about subliminal recordings when I was just beginning to turn my life around. I subscribe to Matt Furey's email list, have for over 12 years as I write this. He sent an email about the power of subliminal recordings. I'm always willing to do everything in my power to grow and become a better person. When I saw the email I thought, "Why not?"

It was the Psycho-Cybernetic Subliminal program by Maxwell Maltz. I was hesitant about the price, over $100.00, but my desire to become a better person is stronger than that. So I bought the—program. Then I waited about four weeks for it to arrive. (This was before audio programs were as easily downloadable as they are today.)

As soon as it showed up in my mailbox, I tore it open, read the directions, and started listening to it. Then the strangest thing happened. I felt agitated, angry. I felt like a caged animal. I wanted to rip off the headphones! But the music was calm and peaceful.

What was going on?

Luckily I'd read about this before. The agitation I was feeling was my subconscious mind fighting these new, empowering messages. The messages of self-confidence and success in the first recording were completely alien beliefs for me. Even though I felt like I was climbing out of my skin, I forced myself to continue listening.

I followed the directions and listened to the first CD two times every day for a month. After the end of the first week I started enjoying the music. The feelings of anger and agitation were replaced by joy, peace, and hope.

That's when I knew it was working.

I felt resistance with each new recording but the time to overcome this grew shorter every time. Since then I've listened to all the recordings countless times. *I cannot imagine where I'd be in life if I'd passed up that opportunity.*

That was one of the best purchases I ever made, period.

Visit this link for a current list of the Best Subliminal Recordings available: http://bit.ly/BestSubliminal

We've discussed why you must make your subconscious mind your ally. We've covered four methods to reprogram your subconscious mind.

1. Affirmations
2. Hypnotherapy
3. Self-Hypnosis
4. Subliminal Recordings

Now let's move on to effectively choosing your destination!

Action Points:

- Turn your subconscious mind into your ally and it will help you achieve your dreams and goals.
- Use these tried and true methods to alter your subconscious beliefs:
    - Affirmations
    - Hypnotherapy
    - Self-Hypnosis
    - Subliminal Recordings

Know Your Destination

The greater danger is not that our hopes are too high and we fail to reach them, it's that they are too low and we do.
—Michelangelo

If you don't know your destination how can you possibly reach it? Often we have only a vague idea of what we want. We might want to help others, to be rich, to be thinner, to have a better job or career, for love in our lives, to do or have all of these things, or for something completely different...

These are fine things to want, to wish for. The problem is that wishes have no real power when it comes to fulfillment. Unless we know exactly what we're after, it's hard to get it.

Think of it this way. Imagine you're in a pitch-black room the size of a football field. You have to locate a spot about five inches square on the West wall and yell, "Eureka!" once you have it. But you haven't anything to help you navigate and you can't see at all. You also have no idea what obstacles might lay in your path. All you know is that from where you stand the West wall is to your left.

What are the chances you'll find the exact spot you're seeking?

Very poor. And that's an understatement. You'd have better odds of being struck by lightning.

What are the chances that you'll end up in the general vicinity of the spot, say a 100 square foot area that touches or contains the five inch square spot you're seeking?

Better. But still slim.

Now, what if the lights are on and you can see all the obstacles, but the wall is a uniform color with nothing to distinguish the spot?

Better still, but it's a big wall. With nothing to distinguish the spot from the rest of the wall you're still relying mostly on luck.

What if the spot is painted bright blue, the lights are on, and you can clearly see all the obstacles?

Almost guaranteed! As long as you do whatever it takes to overcome the obstacles in your path, you'll reach your goal! (Since you're reading this book, I believe you're a person who'll stay the course and do what it takes to succeed.)

That's the difference between having a clear destination—or goal—and having a wish. With a wish you're in the dark, relying on luck. With a clearly defined goal you know your destination and move ahead with confidence.

In both cases you must take action or nothing happens. Even if you can easily see the bright blue spot on the wall, it's not going to come to you. *You must move!*

Since you must first have a clearly defined goal to effectively reach it; let's take care of that now!

Goal Setting

In two of my first seven books, *Your Blueprint: Life by Design* and *Break Your Mold: The Art of Overcoming Patterns and Behaviors That Hold You Back*, I cover goal setting in great detail from the perspective of whole life design. Both books provide step-by-step processes that guide you in redesigning your whole life—and creating changes that last.

In this section we'll focus on effectively setting individual goals. Throughout the book we'll cover all the steps necessary to successfully achieve your goals and how to *apply* the *Law of Action* to the process.

Parts of this section might be review for you. If they are, please do the work anyway. Remember *Action is the secret weapon!*

The first step in successful goal setting is to decide what you want. Simply, you must choose your destination or you'll never reach it.

When you think of your dreams and hopes, what's the thing that comes to mind first, the dream you want more than anything?

Got it?

Great!

Write it here:

_____

When do you want it by? Choose a timeframe that's both realistic and challenging. It needs to be a specific date. If you say, six months from now, then your subconscious mind is satisfied to have the goal be consistently six months away because that's the message you're giving it. When you set an exact date, you have a deadline and a measurable goal.

Write the date for your goal here:

_____

So that's the target, your goal, and when you want to have it. You know where you're going and when you want to get there. That's more than most people when it comes to breathing life into their dreams.

For a goal to be powerful it also needs detail. It's the difference between saying, "I want to go to Alaska someday." and saying, "I want to go to Ketchikan Alaska in the summer of this year, land on the tiny airstrip that is surrounded on three sides by water, and take the ferry across to the town. Then I want to watch the sunset fall across the channel and experience the cruise ships dwarf the tiny shops as they pull up to the pier and tower over the town."

Both goals will get you to Alaska if you focus on them. But only one of the goals has the detail necessary to get you to Ketchikan this summer, where you'll experience all the things mentioned.

Let's use one more example. If your goal is to shed unwanted weight you could say, "I want to drop ten pounds." That's okay. It's a specific number and sets an achievable goal. But what happens when you say it this way, "I want to drop ten pounds and look great in my swimsuit. I love the idea of having toned and healthy muscles that help me to do all the activities I want! I love the thought of seeing definition in my abs and feeling strong and vibrant! I love the way I feel when I exercise and the energy exercising gives me!"

Which feels better? Which goal is more likely to give *you* the motivation to *work out*?

Right; the second one, because *it has detail,* and *detail is power!*

So let's add detail to your goal. Let's *give your goal Power!*

Imagine you've achieved your goal. Think of the wonderful things about succeeding. What's your life like now that you've achieved it? What's different, more exciting? How's life better than where you are now?

In the spaces provided, please write between five and seven things you thought of—about achieving your goal. Choose the things that feel best, that you're most grateful for, and that you're most excited about.

1. _____
   _____
   _____

2. _____

_____

_____

3. _____

_____

_____

4. _____

_____

_____

5. _____

_____

_____

6. _____

_____

_____

7. _____

_____

_____

Did you do it?

Great!

(If not, please *go* back and *do this* exercise because it's critical to the next step.)

Now you know your goal, some things you feel grateful for, and things you're excited about.

Give yourself a pat on the back!

That's more than most people even consider doing. It means you're already one of the elite, one of the few willing to *take action on your dreams!*

Now we'll combine them and create a written goal that's focused like a high-powered laser.

To do this; you'll take your goal, the time frame, the things you're excited about, and those you're grateful for, and then write a paragraph about it.

Here's an example of how it might look:

My Fitness Goal: Workout 5 Days a Week

(Goal Date: *Month Day & Year*)

I'm so happy and grateful now that I exercise 5 times a week. I love the way I feel, the energy I have, and that I'm in better shape every day. I'm grateful for the ways that were presented that allow me have time to exercise. I love taking care of my body and that my body works well and is healthy. It feels wonderful to combine cardio and strength training to optimize my fitness. I love my sense of accomplishment every time I finish a workout. I'm grateful that I feel happier and healthier every day. I love how exercising improves my moods. It feels terrific to wear stylish clothing that accentuates my athletic build and to feel comfortable in my swimsuit.

I'm so happy that I make healthy food choices more and more, and that these, combined with exercising 5 days a week, have renewed my body and spirit!

Using the previous example as a template, write your goal below:

Goal Title: _____

Date: _____

Goal:

_____

_____

_____

_____

_____

_____

_____

_____

_____

_____

_____

_____

_____

_____

_____

_____

_____

_____

_____

_____

Signature: _____

Got it?

Great!

Now that you've taken the actions of choosing your goal, clarifying it, and writing it down, it's time to take the next action step. It's time to really leverage the *Law of Action!*

Review your goal daily! Stand in front of your bathroom mirror and read your goal, visualize it as if it's already happened. Look yourself in the eyes and smile while reading your goal because your eyes are the windows to your soul, your true self.

Finally; as you read, *Be excited. Be energetic.* Allow yourself to *feel* the wonderful emotions of *success*, the *joy, gratitude*, and other feelings that come from realizing your goal.

Do This every day and in no time you'll have amazing changes taking place in your life.

Imagine how you feel now that *you've reached your goal.* Imagine the positive changes that have taken place now that *you've reached your goal.* Imagine all the wonderful things that are now reality now that *you've reached your goal.*

This step might seem silly. But think of it this way. Your new goal is like a seed. You've created it. You dug a hole and planted it. Now it needs sunlight and water to grow. Your emotions of gratitude and joy are like water to your goal. Reviewing it daily is like sunlight. Both are critical.

To make this easier I've created downloadable .pdf worksheets *you* can *use* to *write your goal.* Use the link below to download them. Then print them, fill them out, and tape your goal to your bathroom mirror—or someplace else where you'll see it every morning and night.

Now review your goal every morning before you start your day and every night before you go to bed!

http://bit.ly/My-Goals

And here's the best part, you can *use these worksheets* for all your goals. *I've* just *helped you* release the excuse that you haven't anything to write your goals on. I've also helped you release the excuse of not wanting to write in the book. *You can* also *share* any of the downloadable content from this book—or any of my books—with your family and friends. If *you think it will benefit them*, then *please share it!*

We've covered a lot in this chapter. You've created a goal, written it down, and are reviewing it daily.

That's awesome!

You're taking action on your goals. Do you realize how powerful that is?

I hope you said, "Yes!"

Let's take a break. Come back to the book later to-day or tomorrow and we'll create an action plan for your new goal.

Action Points:
- Without goals dreams are mere wishes
- Clearly defined goals have power
- Use as much detail and as many of your senses as you can when writing your goals
- Review your goals daily

Choose Your Path

"When you're determined to do something,
sometimes you have to take action
and do things you never dreamed of."
— Lou Ferrigno

Now that you've created your goal, the next step is to create a plan for achieving it. *This is a must.* It's a step that many people forget or neglect. As we discussed previously, your plan determines the path that carries you to your goal. Without a plan you can have a goal and take action but still be moving in the wrong direction.

Is that what you want?

Of course not!

However, it's easy to pass on creating your plan. It's easy to think' "I'll do it tomorrow." Or "I don't have time right now." Or, "I can reach my goal without a plan."

You know what those thoughts are?

They're your subconscious mind working overtime to talk you out of taking action on your goal!

Just last night I was working with a dear friend who is desperate to change the state of his life. He was asking for my advice and said he's ready to do anything necessary to change his life. In the end we agreed that he'd start with creating a two week goal. He'd write it and email it to me for review before the end of the day.

His subconscious mind isn't so keen on changing his life though.

How do I know?

You guessed it!

I never got the email.

When I asked him why he never sent it, he said he got home and lost track of time until it was too late to write it.

When I asked him to do it today he responded, "If I have time I will."

That's how powerful our subconscious minds are.

We can have the best intentions, but unless we work on our core subconscious beliefs we'll have a hard time changing our lives. The subconscious mind is like a mule, stubborn, it'll dig in its heels until you convince it that what you want is really what it wants too...

That's why it's critical you *use the techniques* in the chapter *Your Subconscious Mind* to align your subconscious beliefs with your conscious goals.

Do you feel any internal push-back when it comes to creating your plan? *Do It Anyway!*

Tell any thought that tries to distract you from creating your plan, "Thank you for your input." And then *create your plan anyway!*

Do you sense the theme here?

Things might come up that interfere with you making your plan. You might have distractions. You might feel like it's okay to put it off until tomorrow or that you'll do it when you know how to *create a plan*. You might even forget what you were doing and remember later.

Create Your Plan Anyway!

When thoughts like these show up, it's critical that you *keep moving forward* and *Take Action!*

Create Your Plan Anyway!

Taking action in spite of distraction sends a clear message to your subconscious mind that what you're doing is important! It's a great way to start creating an action habit. And that's a great habit to have.

So what are you gonna do?

Right; *Create Your Plan Anyway!*

If you're new to planning, creating a plan might feel overwhelming. That's okay. Your plan doesn't need to be complex. In fact, the simpler the plan the better because simpler things are easier to complete.

Your plan needs a few parts to be effective:
- Daily and Weekly Steps
- Check Points
- Sign Posts
- Feedback

Daily and Weekly Steps

For your action plan to work, you must think about what you need to do to reach your goal.

When you know what you're going to do, what daily steps you must take, you're better able to make consistent progress in the right direction. Your plan can be to take action, any action, but it's more effective if you know the specific actions you're going to take because it helps you stay focused on the goal.

Daily Steps are things you need to do every day to successfully achieve your goal. If you're unsure what your daily steps might be, then ask yourself, "What things, when compounded daily, will best carry me toward my destination?"

For example; I'm writing this book. Writing a book can feel daunting to say the least. But I've written a few. (You can find them here: http://www.rolandbyrd.co/books-by-roland-byrd/).

I know that as long as I show up every day and write, I'll eventually finish the book. I've also learned that having a daily writing goal works best because it's a definite and measurable target. Without a definite, measurable target it's easy to say, "I wrote a sentence." Or, "I wrote a paragraph, so I'm good for the day."

It takes a very long time to write a book if you're only producing a sentence or paragraph a day... I know. The books I've approached that way are either still unfinished or took a very long time to write and rewrite.

My daily goal for this book is 500 words a day. That's an easily achievable goal. I've hit or exceeded it most days since starting this project. And I've fallen short a few days. But I *show up every day*, aim for that target, and *make progress*.

Every goal can be broken down into daily steps. Your fitness goal's daily steps might be working out every day for a minimum of 30 minutes and deciding what types, and how much, food you'll eat. Daily steps for your financial goal might be how much you'll save, invest, spend, or earn every day. A scholastic goal can be broken down into how much time you'll study every day. A spiritual goal can be broken down into things like meditating, studying scripture and religious texts, and praying daily.

You get the idea.

Now let's do this!

For the goal you wrote down earlier, write your daily action steps here:

I've provided ten spaces. You can use them all if you'd like. If you have fewer than ten daily steps, that's okay too.

My Daily Action Steps

1. _____
   _____
   _____

2. _____
   _____
   _____

3. _____
   _____
   _____

4. _____
   _____
   _____

5. _____
   _____
   _____

6. _____
   _____

_____

7. _____

_____

_____

8. _____

_____

_____

9. _____

_____

_____

10. _____

_____

_____

Now that you've written down your daily action steps, let's write your weekly action steps. Weekly action steps are things you must do once a week that move you closer to your goal.

One of my weekly action steps is to fill out my weekly planning form. This helps me plan my week and helps me stay focused as I work my daily action list. I've created a weekly planning form for you to download and use.

http://bit.ly/WeeklyPlanningForm

Another of my weekly action steps is to send an email to those on my email list. If I send email every day it might get annoying to the people who *subscribe to my newsletter*. Once or twice a week is okay though. By adding this to my weekly action steps I have a much higher likelihood of actually doing it.

Every goal has things that make sense to do once a week. For a fitness goal it might be to weigh yourself, to check your body fat percentage, or to have a cheat day on your diet. For a financial goal if might be to calculate the returns on your investments. For a spiritual goal it might be fasting one day—going without food—while seeking spiritual unity or instruction. You might also rest from your normal daily labors on Sunday—to help make the day more sacred on a personal level. For a scholastic goal it might be to review your class notes.

Think of your goal. Now ask yourself, "What things can I do once a week that will move me closer to realizing my goal?"

Got a few?

Great!

Please write them here:

My Weekly Action Steps

1. _____
   _____
   _____

2. _____
   _____
   _____

3. _____
   _____
   _____

4. _____
   _____
   _____

5. _____
   _____
   _____

Way to go!

Now you've written your daily and weekly action steps. That means *You're Taking Action!* And you're well on your way to having a powerful action plan.

It's time to move to the next part of your action plan.

Checkpoints

Checkpoints are a way of measuring your progress over time. They help you know whether you're *taking effective action* or just taking action. Think of your checkpoints like a measuring tape or mini goals.

Imagine you've shrunk to the size of an ant. Your goal is to go twenty-five feet so you can reach the device that'll make you normal sized again. Your checkpoints could be to travel twenty-four inches every minute. That way you'll reach your goal in twelve and a half minutes.

Checkpoints also allow you to monitor your progress. If you're not at the first checkpoint in one minute then you know you're moving too slowly and you can step it up. If you reach your first checkpoint in under one minute then perhaps you underestimated your abilities and you can adjust your checkpoints so you reach your goal faster.

For example; my first checkpoint for writing this book is to have the first draft completed fourteen days from now. My next checkpoint is to have the first run edit completed within ten days of that.

Effective checkpoints are time based and measurable. Otherwise they have no real power. Which do you think is more likely to drive me to massive action? Saying "I'll complete my first draft of this book this year." Or saying, "I'll complete my first draft of this book in fourteen days." The first one creates a lot less motivation. The second one really lights the fire!

It's the same for your goals. Create checkpoints that are realistic *and* challenging. Challenging checkpoints create urgency. Urgency feeds motivation and invites massive action.

For a fitness goal your checkpoints could be based on capabilities or results. Using capabilities you could have a checkpoint of doing twenty-five pushups in a row by a certain date. Using results you could have a checkpoint of dropping two inches off your waist size by a certain date.

The checkpoints you use work best if you're basing them on the type of goal you have. If your goal is focused on getting leaner, then checkpoints based on body measurements make more sense than ones based on how many reps of an exercise you can do. Likewise, if your goal is focused on strength, endurance, or muscularity then it makes more sense to base your checkpoints on the number of reps you can do or the time and speed of an activity like sprinting, bike riding, or running.

For a scholastic goal your checkpoints could be things like getting a certain grade on an upcoming test, maintaining a certain GPA, or getting accepted into the University, College, or other program of your choice.

For a financial goal your checkpoints could be how much money you've saved or invested by a certain date. They could also be how much average return you're getting on your investments, maintaining a positive balance in your bank account, or consistently paying your bills on time.

For a spiritual goal your checkpoints could be a streak of days where you meditate, pray—or both—every day. It could be increasing your time meditating to twenty minutes. A Spiritual checkpoint could be finishing a chapter or book of scripture, or other spiritual texts by a certain time. Another spiritual checkpoint could be to successfully fast for twenty-four hours by a certain date or to experience a more spiritually meaningful fast.

As you realize, your checkpoints will vary based on your goal but effective checkpoints are always attainable based on consistent action. They are also measurable. That way you can tell how close you've come to them or how far *you exceeded your expectations.*

You understand the power of checkpoints so let's create a few for your goal:

My Checkpoints

1. _____
_____
_____
_____

2. _____
_____
_____
_____

3. _____
_____
_____
_____

4. _____
_____
_____
_____

So far in this chapter you've created your daily and weekly action steps and you've created checkpoints to help you measure your progress. Do you realize how amazing you are?

Seriously. Many people want to change their lives, few are willing to take the action necessary to do it. Even fewer understand how to apply the *Law of Action!* The fact that you're reading this book *and* taking action is wonderful.

Always remember that. And always remember:

You are Wonderful!

You are Amazing!

You can do anything you set your mind to!

I'll remind you of this throughout the book because we all can use a cheerleader at times.

Signposts

Signposts are similar to checkpoints because they help you measure your progress. Where they differ is that they aren't things you plan ahead of time. Signposts are events or happenings that verify you're on the right path. When you're working out regularly and someone tells you how great you look, that's a signpost. When you're studying diligently and a friend or teacher tells you that you seem to really grasp the material, that's a signpost.

Signposts can also be opportunities to change course and often better fulfill your purpose.

When I wrote my first book, *Your Blueprint: Life by Design*, I'd struggled through the first thirty pages. It seemed I fought for every word. Then one day I was browsing my local book store when my eyes were drawn to *Hypnotic Writing* by Dr. Joe Vitale. Trusting that I'd been led to the book, I bought it. Over the next two days I read the book and took copious notes.

Hypnotic Writing was a signpost for me. It was a message to change the way I write. From it I learned how to turn off my internal editor and just let the first draft flow. I also learned how to engage my subconscious mind in my writing process and trust inspiration.

I completed the entire first draft of *Your Blueprint: Life by Design* within ten days by applying the methods I learned from that book. Reading *Hypnotic Writing*, acknowledging its message, and taking action on it improved my writing beyond measure! Even now I use the knowledge I gained from it in all of my writing.

Thank you Dr. Joe!

Since you're just starting your action plan, you may not have recognized any signposts yet. That's okay! Once you're open to them you'll start seeing them.

When you recognize a signpost first ask, "What does this tell me?" Then ask, "How do I apply this?"

As you know, signposts can tell you you're on the right path. They can also tell you something must change. When they affirm you're on the right path, keep doing what you're doing! When they tell you something must change, simply adjust your actions. I've discovered that the messages that something must change often allow me to achieve even better results than my original plan would have. Then they help me surpass my goal!

So when you come across a signpost that guides you to modify your approach, accept it with an open heart.

Here are few spaces to document your signposts as they appear.

Signposts:

1. _____

   _____

   _____

   _____

   a. What does this tell me?

   b. How will I apply this?

2. _____

a. What does this tell me?

_____

_____

_____

_____

b. How will I apply this?

_____

_____

_____

_____

3. _____

_____

_____

_____

a. What does this tell me?

_____

_____

_____

_____

b. How will I apply this?

_____

_____

_____

_____

4. _____

   _____

   _____

   _____

    a. What does this tell me?

   _____

   _____

   _____

   _____

    b. How will I apply this?

   _____

   _____

   _____

   _____

When you receive a signpost that significantly alters the action you're taking toward your goal, it's best to revisit and modify the daily and weekly steps in your action plan. That ensures you're implementing the new information. Otherwise it's easy to go back to your routine without implementing your new knowledge. That's as good as ignoring the signpost!

Since you're in this to *Take Action and Reach Your Goal* you understand the value in changing course when needed.

Now for the final piece in an effective action plan!

Feedback

Feedback is similar to signposts because it tells us how we're doing as we work toward our goal. But feedback is more subtle. Signposts are major markers that can dramatically affirm or alter our course, feedback helps us assess how our daily actions are working. Signposts are also less frequent while feedback is usually a daily occurrence.

Feedback aids in minor course corrections, like the minute corrections you make when driving. You see, hear, and feel changes in the road—or obstacles ahead—and accelerate, decelerate, or steer around them. You'd never let go of the wheel and expect to stay on course! Feedback toward successfully achieving your goal is the same. Pay attention to it and correct course as needed.

When you reach, exceed, or fall short of your checkpoints, that's feedback! Those are messages that your approach is either working, working better than you'd anticipated, or that it needs to be modified.

If you have a fitness goal and the day after a workout you're so sore you can hardly move, that's feedback. It's your body telling you to lighten up a bit.

If you have a spiritual goal to feel more peace and you feel disconnected or agitated instead of peaceful, those could be messages that you need to meditate or pray more often. They could also be symptoms that there is someone you must forgive to achieve deeper peace in your life or that something else in your life is creating discord.

If you have a financial goal to make an average ten percent return on your investments but you're consistently losing money instead, that's feedback! Perhaps you should change your method or learn more ways to invest.

If you have a scholastic goal and you seem to struggle grasping some concepts you're studying, that's feedback that your study techniques might need altering.

Here's an example:

Spelling

My son, Gary, is ten as I write this. Recently we discovered that he was struggling with his spelling. He is very intelligent, yet his spelling test scores were far below what we know he's capable of. That was feedback that something was amiss.

With Gary's agreement, we implemented a simple study technique. Twice a week we review his spelling words. Gary and I sit six or seven feet apart. I tell him a word from his weekly spelling list and toss him a rugby ball. He spells the word and tosses the ball back. If he gets the word right I congratulate him and we move to the next word. If he misses the word we discuss the error and find ways to associate the word to something—an action or idea—that helps the correct spelling mentally stick.

For example, with the word "explosion" I might have Gary crouch down and then jump up and throw his arms wide as he spells it. Or I might have him think of a firecracker and how it explodes with a bang.

Then we try again.

Once he gets the word right we spell it a few more times, to help anchor the correct spelling, and then move to the next word.

The entire process takes less than twenty minutes. Total time invested in spelling study is less than forty minutes a week. Since starting this method his spelling scores have skyrocketed! And more importantly, Gary is starting to believe that he is good at spelling.

This has the added benefits of being a fun activity that lets Gary know he's important enough for my wife Vauna and me to notice he needed help and for me to take the time to work with him. It also helps him learn memory techniques—associating things when studying and including multiple senses to anchor them—which will only help as he moves through life.

What if Vauna and I hadn't received the feedback that Gary needed help with his spelling or worse, hadn't paid attention to it when we saw it?

Then Gary would probably still be struggling and, sadly, reinforcing a mistaken belief about his spelling skills.

Feedback also can be internal, a feeling or knowing that something must change. When you're working toward a goal and you feel inspired to do—or avoid—something related to your goal, that's feedback too.

Here are few spaces to document the feedback you're getting.

Feedback:

1. _____

   _____

   _____

   _____

   a. What does this tell me?

      _____

      _____

      _____

      _____

   b. How will I apply this?

      _____

      _____

      _____

      _____

2. _____

   _____

   _____

   _____

a. What does this tell me?

_____

_____

_____

_____

b. How will I apply this?

_____

_____

_____

_____

3. _____

_____

_____

_____

a. What does this tell me?

_____

_____

_____

_____

b. How will I apply this?

_____

_____

_____

_____

4. _____
   _____
   _____
   _____

   a. What does this tell me?

     _____
     _____
     _____
     _____

   b. How will I apply this?

     _____
     _____
     _____
     _____

As you pay attention to the feedback you're getting, and adjust accordingly, it becomes easier to recognize it and act on it. Soon it becomes a habit and just like driving, you're making course corrections automatically!

Action Points:
- Download your Action Plan Worksheets:
- http://bit.ly/MyActionPlan
- An Action Plan is essential to achieving your goal

- An effective Action Plan includes:
  - Daily and Weekly Steps
  - Check Points
  - Sign Posts
  - Feedback

Overcoming Inertia

"People that won't take step number 1,
never take step number 2."
—Zig Ziglar

You understand the importance of the Law of Action. *Nothing happens without action.* Action transforms your dreams and goals from wishes to reality. You understand that actions can be mental or physical. You've created your goal. You've created your action plan. *You're taking focused action.*

You've already taken step number one! You're also creating new habits. You're making steady progress. And *you're just getting started!*

Remember the Law of Action:

Nothing Happens Without Action!

You Must Take Action to Realize Your Dreams!

The truth is; the need for action never ceases. You're always taking actions. Even before discovering the *Law of Action* you were taking action every day, if you're alive and conscious you're taking action. The crux is those actions probably weren't carrying you consistently closer to your goals and dreams. Chances are they were random, even unconscious, with little to no direction from you.

As you know, a life of random, unconscious actions creates people who are cause and effect mechanisms. That's life but not living! People who live that way aren't consciously creating their life, they're existing instead of living. They're simply reacting to everything that happens. They're like ships with no sail, motor, keel, rudder, or captain, tossed about hopelessly on the stormy seas of life.

Is that how you choose to live?

I didn't think so.

Now it's time to *put your action plan in motion!* To do that you must overcome inertia.

The Law of Inertia: *An object at rest will remain at rest unless acted on by an *unbalanced force. An object in motion continues in motion with the same speed and in the same direction unless acted upon by an unbalanced force.* (*An unbalanced force is a force that disturbs the equilibrium of the object—changes the direction of motion or the momentum of the object.)

You must start moving because a body at rest stays at rest. Unless *you take action* and start moving toward your goal, you're going to remain still. Or something else, an external force unrelated to your desires, will act on you and move you in the wrong direction.

That'll never get you what you want.

Once you start moving toward your goals and dreams, that's when the magic starts because a body in motion stays in _____!

Right! *A body in motion stays in motion.*

When you're in motion, you build momentum and momentum creates miracles. When it comes to your goal—and the direction of your life—momentum is the cumulative energy that carries you forward. Every action you take adds momentum. Some actions add a little and some are a giant push, but they all increase the energy that's fulfilling your goal.

It's true, it takes more energy to start moving than it does to keep moving. That means it's going to take more effort on your part to get moving toward your goals than it will to keep moving toward them. But it also means that once you're moving toward your goals, it takes less effort to keep moving toward them.

Here's a secret. If you keep applying the same energy to your goals after you're moving, that you did when you started, it dramatically increases your speed.

The good news is that *you're already in motion!* You're reading the Law of Action! You're doing the exercises! You're consciously using the Law of Action in your life! You're already taking consistent action *and* building momentum!

That's Awesome!

Keep at it!

Now is a critical time in the realization of your goals. It's easy to think, "I'm already taking action and making progress. I can ease off a little and still make it."

Avoid that trap! It steals momentum.

To successfully realize your goal you must *make daily action a habit*. Otherwise you'll lose momentum, slow down. You might even stop.

Sometimes we take consistent action for a while. Then we get distracted by other things in life or things aren't happening fast enough for us, so we stop taking consistent action toward our goal.

What happens then?

Right!

We slow down. Eventually we stop moving forward. Then our goal becomes a disappointing memory of what we thought we could accomplish. Often we use this as evidence to support disempowering beliefs about our abilities. Damaging labels like Failure or Quitter get thrown around. We might rationalize that we didn't really want the dream anyway...so we can feel better about giving up.

There is nothing sadder than a person who's given up on their dreams. When a person gives up on their dreams they're really giving up on themselves.

Sometimes they give up because they didn't understand how to achieve their dreams or they don't believe they deserve them. Sometimes it's because they lack belief in their abilities or worse, they listened to well-meaning people who tried to protect them by telling them their dreams were impossible.

Here are a few simple rules to help you avoid these traps. They'll also help you build and maintain momentum as you bring your goals and dreams to life.

- When you don't feel like working on your goal because you're tired or discouraged:
  - Work on it anyway.
- When you feel like you're not making progress:
  - Work on your goal anyway.
- When someone tells you to give up on your dream because _____, (insert their negative comment):
  - Tell them, "Thank you for your input." and then work on your goal anyway.
- When your own brain tells you to give up on your dream because of _____:
  - Tell your mind, "Thank you for your input." and then work on your goal anyway.
- When you feel overwhelmed, anxious, or like you're not good enough:
  - Think of ten things you're grateful for, write them down, and then work on your goal anyway.

I never said this was easy. It's not always puppies, kittens, sunshine, and rainbows. If it was, everyone would have complete success in all areas of their life. But *you can do this!* You can *achieve your goals.* You're miles ahead because *you're taking action!*

But not just any action will do. Remember the analogy of hacking away in the wrong jungle? Your daily actions must move you toward your goal. Otherwise they're wasted effort and possibly hurting your progress.

Now, understand that not all of your daily actions will carry you closer to your goals. Many of them will be unrelated to your goals and dreams. When we're discussing taking focused actions, I'm referring to the *time you spend every day working on your goals and dreams.* That might be thirty minutes, it might be an hour or two, or it might be longer. The critical distinction is this; *the time you spend working on your goal or dream must be focused—no distractions—and the actions you take during that time must move you closer to your goal.*

Period.

What does that have to do with momentum?

Great question.

Imagine you're tasked with moving a huge log that's lying across the road. It's blocking traffic and people are getting angry. But it's your job to move it.

You walk up to it, examine it, and then see a robin. Its red breast seems to glow, its head bobs, and its eyes twinkle as it hops around on the ground nearby. It flies to a tree that's just inside the forest. You really want a picture of it, so you pull your phone out of your pocket and follow the robin into the woods.

The robin keeps darting from tree to tree. You chase it. You finally get close enough to take its picture. That done, you remember the log and wander back to the road. By this time the people are really angry. The line of cars stretches as far as you can see. Horns are blaring, people are screaming, and no-one is offering to help.

You try to calm the people down. But it doesn't work. So you shake your head and walk back up to the log. You try to figure out how to move it but are having trouble thinking of a way. Then you notice a buck in the woods with a six-point rack. The deer stares at you, like it wants your attention. Forgetting about the log you follow the buck into the woods hoping to get its picture...

Seem ridiculous?

That's how many of us spend our time working on our goals and dreams. The log is the task we need to accomplish to move to our next step. But we allow ourselves to get distracted again and again. Things that should take minutes to accomplish end up taking hours or worse, not getting done at all.

When you take hours to accomplish a few minutes' worth of work, what does that do to your momentum?

Yeah, it kills it!

Here's another way the scenario could unfold:

You're tasked with moving a huge log that's lying across the road. It's blocking traffic and people are getting angry. But it's your job to move it.

You examine the log and realize it's too big for you to move on you own. So you stand on top of the log, motion for people's attention, and make an announcement.

"I need help from the strongest drivers in line. If we work together we can easily move this log!"

Within minutes a group of strong drivers has gathered. Working together you move the log off the roadway. You thank them, everyone involved gets back in their cars and goes on their way.

The robin was still there. The buck was there too. You never noticed them because you were focused on the task you needed to accomplish!

That's what removing distractions and taking focused actions accomplishes. *It gets the work done.*

Then you can move to the next step, the next action.

What does that do to your momentum?

It builds on it because you're taking actions that move you closer to your goal instead of flitting randomly about chasing butterflies—or robins and bucks in this case.

4 Keys to Overcoming Inertia.

1. Set time aside every day to work on your goal.
2. Remove all distractions possible when working on your goal.
3. Before taking action ask yourself, "Does this move me closer to my goal?"
4. Pay attention to what's working and do more of that!

Let's examine each of these in more detail.

Golden Time

Set Time Aside Every Day to Work on Your Goal

This is critical. Your goals and dreams aren't going to fulfil themselves. They require what? _____

Right! *Action* on your part. If you aren't willing to set aside, or make time to work on your goal every day, then how can you take consistent action?

You've heard many people bemoan the fact that they haven't reached their goals or that they have dreams that are unattainable. Of those people, how many have you heard use the excuse that they don't have the time to work on their dreams?

Most of them, if not all.

Lack of time is one of the biggest excuses out there. It's easy to blame lack of time and a busy schedule for our inability to create the success we desire.

Do you know any people who use this excuse? Do you know any of them personally? Have you perhaps used this excuse from time to time? I know I have. I used to think I didn't have time to work on my dreams. So my dreams remained dreams—with little hope of actualization.

Then I started making time to work on my dreams, making that time a priority. And an amazing thing happened. My dreams started coming true!

Understand, what the excuse, "I don't have time to work on my dreams," really means is, "I'd rather spend my time doing something else."

I know, Ouch!

But it's true.

Since you're reading this book I know *you're ready to take Action* on your dreams and goals. So I'm going to tell you something that I'm positive you can handle.

In almost all cases, someone who doesn't have time to work on their dreams and goals really has either a time management problem or a priority problem.

How can I say that?

If they truly wanted to work on their goals and dreams, they'd *find a way.*

That might seem harsh. I know most of us feel that our time is maxed out. What I'm referring to is the fact that we all have bubbles of wasted time during our days. Some have huge bubbles and some have small bubbles, but all of us have time we're wasting, time we could redirect toward our goals and dreams.

Consider this. How much time does the average person spend watching TV or movies? How much time do you spend surfing the internet? How much time do you spend on social media sites like Facebook, Google+, Twitter, Pinterest, LinkedIn, Tsu, Instagram, etc? How much time do you spend playing computer or console games?

Is that time helping you move closer to your goals and dreams? Is it helping you grow as a person? Is it helping others?

That behavior is indicative of both a priority problem and a time management problem. Choosing to make things like social media and entertainment more important than goals and dreams is priority misalignment. And using time that could be used on goals and dreams to goof off equates to time management issues.

Yes, entertainment is important and play is important. We all need time to unwind and leisure time—otherwise why are we working so hard? But unchecked entertainment—internet, TV, movies, gaming, etc.—isn't healthy. Endless hours of TV, movies, gaming, and social media is escapism. It's addictive. It's zoning out from reality. Worse, it's the choice to live stuck in your present situation instead of doing something to change it!

The point is this. If you think you haven't time to work on your dreams and goals every day, then perhaps it's time to take a close look at the way you use your time. If you make the choice to spend one hour less on play or entertainment, then that's an hour you can easily dedicate to your dreams and goals.

You'll be amazed how much you'll accomplish if you dedicate even an hour every day to your goal and dreams!

My friend, mentor, and hall of fame speaker Patrick Combs (http://patrickcombs.com) calls dedicating an hour a day to your goals and dreams *Golden Time*. He introduced me to it years ago and honestly, it's how I've written over 8 books!

Golden Time means dedicating an hour a day to your dreams and goals. The secret is to remove all distractions during your Golden Time.

No email. No phone. No surfing the Internet.

Work exclusively on your current action step—of a goal related to your dream.

Yes, that means *you must have a goal*!

An hour a day is an insignificant amount of time to set aside. It's small enough that most anyone who wants to can find a way to do it. But when you add those hours up, that's the magic!

One hour a day, over the course of a year, is equivalent to 8 weeks of work at a day job! That's two months of work!

What will you accomplish when you give two months of dedicated, focused attention to your goals and dreams this coming year?

Starting on the next page I'll reveal how to get the most out of your Golden Time.

Remove All Distractions Possible When Working on Your Goal.

Distractions steal momentum. They're dream killers. Every time you shift focus from one thing to another, it takes time. When you notice and act on distractions, it not only shifts your focus, it can derail your thoughts, making it difficult to get back on task when you decide to leave the distraction.

Life's full of distractions. The trick is to remove all possible distractions *and* to train yourself to ignore those you can't remove. This might seem difficult at first. But it gets easier with repetition.

First we must identify our personal distractions. Once we know what they are, we can more easily remove them while we're working on our goals and dreams. The following things might be distractions—and are easy to remove temporarily.

- Email
- Instant Messaging
- Social Media
- Cellphones
- TV
- Internet
- Talk Radio

- Gossip
- Online Games

The nature of the distraction depends on the type of work you're doing to bring your dream to life. If you're mostly working on a computer—as I do—then things like email, instant messaging, and social media can be huge distractions. With discipline these can be ignored. You can also close the applications or turn off your Internet connection when it's not needed. That might sound extreme, but most programs don't require the Internet to function and if there isn't an active Internet connection no emails or instant messages will come in.

When you're finished with your daily, dedicated time then you can turn them back on.

If your goal or dream requires you to work with others, gossip can be a distraction, not to mention the negative influence gossip has. How can you work on bettering yourself if you're busy professing other's weaknesses?

"Gossip is the Devils radio." — George Harrison

Talking about current events, unrelated to your goals, also wastes time. Listening to talk radio when you're supposed to work on your goals and dreams is a distraction. Many talk radio shows are steeped in negativity. Allowing yourself to work in a negative atmosphere is like throwing a wet blanket on the fire of your success. At best it'll dampen the fire. At worst it'll smother it.

Instrumental music, classical music, or white noise types are okay because they provide relaxing background noise. But music with lyrics and talk shows make it hard to focus wholly on your task. When your attention is split, between lyrics or a talk show host's chatter and what you're trying to work on, you're much less effective.

Regardless of the work you're doing toward your goals and dreams, cell phones are a huge distraction—especially now that email, the Internet, and social media are on smart phones and begging for attention. It's best to turn off your ringer—or even your phone—while you're working on your goals and dreams. If your phone must stay on, then disable notifications from your social media apps and email!

A good measure when determining if something is a distraction is to ask yourself this question, "Is this helping my goal or dream?"

If the answer is, "No." Then avoid it during your Golden Time.

Before Taking Action Ask Yourself, "Does This Move Me Closer to My Goal?"

It's possible to build momentum in the wrong direction. As you realize, that steals momentum from your goal because the energy you could apply to your goal is going somewhere else. If the actions you're taking aren't moving you closer to the successful realization of your goal, then they're the wrong actions to take when you're working on your goal.

This ties in with distractions. The difference is you can take valuable actions that aren't associated with the goal or dream you're working on. Understand, there's nothing wrong with those action themselves, they just need to be done at a different time. Even if the actions are things you need to do, or are helpful for other things you're working on, if they're not aligned with the specific goal or dream you're working on, they can, and should wait.

If your goal is to write a book about cooking healthy meals and you're using your dedicated time to research how to build a better canoe, or you're cleaning the garage... Those are the wrong actions. If you're goal is to get healthy and fit and you're using your dedicated time to watch videos about how to invest your money better... Yeah, wrong action.

You must be protective of your Golden Time—the time you've set aside to work on your goal and dream. That means protecting that time from distractions, from other people who might derail your actions, and from yourself using it for other purposes. (So make sure you schedule your Golden Time during a part of your day that minimizes or removes these conflicts. I personally use the time between 5:00am and 6:30am every day.)

During your Golden Time, always keep the question in mind, "Does this move me closer to my goal?"

Use that question as the litmus test against all the actions you take. If you want to do something but it doesn't move you closer to your goal, then it's a distraction. You should either avoid it entirely or set it aside until later.

Got it?

Great!

Pay Attention to What's Working and Do More of That

This might seem like a no-brainer, but you'd be amazed how many people aren't paying attention to the results they're getting. This is feedback plain and simple. When you aren't paying attention to your feedback you won't be able to build on your success. Building on success is one of the fastest ways to build momentum. And momentum creates what?

Right. *Momentum creates miracles!*

First, open yourself to feedback. Then watch, listen, and feel the messages the feedback is giving you. Take those lessons and use them to improve your actions, and yourself.

When feedback tells you an action is really working, do more of it! You can also fine tune the action and get even better results.

Paying attention to your results allows you to discover what's working. Discovering what's working allows you to build on those actions. Building on actions that are working allow you to increase momentum. Increasing momentum skyrockets your ability to successfully achieve your goal!

You can do this!

Now that you're mastering the art of overcoming inertia and building momentum, let's discuss the power of taking inspired action.

Action Points:
- The need for Action never ceases
- Give time and attention to your goals and dreams daily
- Remove distractions while working on your goals and dreams
- As little as one hour a day gives you the equivalent of two months (at 40 hrs a week) working on your goal every year

Take Inspired Action

"If one advances confidently in the direction of his dreams, and endeavors to live the life which he has imagined, he will meet with a success unexpected in common hours."
—Henry David Thoreau

Inspired action is a powerful force when working on your goals and dreams. Inspiration comes in many forms and should never be ignored. Many times you'll make intuitive leaps that defy reason but still give you all the information you need to move to the next step.

When you're working on your goal, there are times you'll have a strong feeling you should do something related to your goal. You may even have a strong feeling you should do something seemingly unrelated to your goal.

Trust these feelings. Take action on them.

Your intuition, your gut instinct has access to information you're not consciously aware of. It has everything in your subconscious mind at its fingertips. It also has access to the energy field that binds all humanity, some call this the universal mind. I also believe your intuition connects you to God and allows you to receive personal revelation.

Your intuition never lies or misleads you. It's often described as a knowing, an indisputable knowledge or feeling that you must take an action. It can be subtle, like a whisper in your mind. At times, when you have an intuitive thought, it's like a powerful realization or perhaps a tingling feeling accompanies it, like you're immersed in a shower of harmless electricity.

What's the power of intuition? Here are two examples where I listened to my intuition and it had life changing results:

Where's Auriana?

The thought hit me from nowhere. I had to find my four year old daughter. Now! I asked my wife, Vauna, "Have you seen Auri?"

"No. She was just here." She replied looking puzzled.

We were at a company picnic. Hundreds of people mulled around in conversation. Activities were scattered around the park. There were many places for a young child to get lost. And Auri was an adventurous child. She had no fear.

"I've got to find her." I said. I started walking briskly, almost jogging, along the edge of the long building, scanning the crowd as I went. It felt like I was being pulled forward. So I didn't slow to look. I followed my knowing that I needed to keep moving forward.

I came to the building's corner. Instantly I knew to turn left and follow the wall. A few moments later I came to the next corner. *Turn left*, I felt. So I did.

I looked down the length of the building and immediately saw a small child tumble over the five foot high wall of the dunk-tank into the water.

Auri!

I sprinted to the tank and leapt as high as I could. I simultaneously landed with my stomach on the top of the tank wall, grabbed the edge with my left hand, and lunged headfirst into the cold water. I grabbed a handful of Auri's shirt with my right hand and yanked her up—out of the water and over the wall—to safety.

Then I cried. So did Auri. I'd pulled her out of the water within one second of her falling in. She was safe. Wet and cold, but safe.

There were at least fifty people within a few seconds of the dunk-tank. Not one of them had known anything was wrong. Not one of them had seen my daughter climb the ladder on the outside of the tank or watched as she lost her balance and fell in.

I'd been nearly three-hundred feet away, on the far side of the long building when I'd had the feeling that I must find Auri. If I'd have ignored that feeling because I was in a conversation, hesitated even a moment before trying to find her, or second guessed which way to turn, I wouldn't have seen her fall into the tank.

I would have been too late.

Understand, there was no ladder on the inside of the tank. It had smooth walls and was full of cold water. Auri would have drowned. But she's alive today, a beautiful, intelligent nineteen year old with the world at her fingertips, because I listened to my intuition.

Is there something special about me that allows me to receive intuitive guidance?

No.

We all have this ability. You have it. Your neighbor has it. Your best friend has it. Even those you dislike have it. The secret is to *train yourself to listen.*

Here's another time listening to my intuition had amazing results.

Get Your Cargo Net

A few years ago I had a motorcycle accident. I was hit by a minivan on the freeway while traveling about 55 mph. You can read the full account of the incident in my contribution to the bestselling book, *The Prosperity Factor*—with Dr. Joe Vitale.

Here's the rest of the story.

That morning, when I found out I needed to go to a client that was an hour's ride away, I felt the strong urge to stop by my house and get my motorcycle's cargo net.

While working as a Network Engineer, I had a computer backpack—full of my tools and my laptop. It weighed nearly thirty pounds. That's not a lot of weight, but it's enough to change your center of gravity.

I always wear full gear on my motorcycle—helmet, boots, armored jacket, armored gloves, etc. And I usually wore my computer pack like a backpack when riding my motorcycle for work. It was easier, and faster, than taking the time to strap the bag down.

But that day I felt I should use my cargo net instead. So I went home, quickly found the cargo net, and strapped my computer bag to the back of my motorcycle.

The trip to the client was uneventful. On the way home I was merging onto the freeway when I was hit by the minivan. I was launched into the air at about 55mph.

Instinctively I tucked-and-rolled down the freeway. Then I slammed into a road-marker. That stopped me. I ended up with a broken wrist, a bruised lower back, lots of other bumps and bruises, and a shoulder that eventually needed surgery to repair.

I was able to tuck-and-roll because my computer pack was strapped to the back of my bike. If I hadn't listened to my intuition, to the prompting to get my cargo net, my center of gravity would have been off. I couldn't have tucked-and-rolled effectively. Instead of a compact shape rolling down the freeway, dispersing momentum, I'd have tumbled wildly in a tangle of limbs.

I shudder to think what would have happened if I'd rag-dolled down the freeway at 55mph...

These two events were life-changing. They're extreme examples of the benefits of listening to intuition because the results were dramatic and far reaching. Most of the time you may never know what would have happened if you didn't listen. You just know something is different, less than it would have been had you listened.

Once you're used to receiving intuitive guidance, you'll realize these messages guide you in all areas of your life. They help you navigate difficult situations and can keep you from danger. They also help you achieve better results than you thought possible when it comes to your goals and dreams.

The trick is getting to the place where you can identify these feelings. If you're unable to identify intuitive guidance, how can you act on it? When you have a lot of internal noise or discord, it hampers your ability to hear, feel, or see the guidance your intuition is offering.

How do you quiet your mind and open yourself to receiving the messages your intuition is sending?

The best way I've discovered to open myself to receiving intuitive guidance is through daily meditation. Since I'm deeply religious, I also pray daily. The combination of the two is very powerful. For me, meditation is like listening to creation and prayer is talking to God. Whether or not you're religious, meditation stills your mind and opens you to receiving intuitive guidance.

I recommend both prayer and meditation. Do what works best for you, of course. If you aren't religious, that's okay, intuitive guidance is still available to you.

I'm offering my process for receiving intuitive guidance. At a minimum I recommend daily meditation because it helps quiet your mind, heightens your intellect, and opens you to receiving these messages.

When I pray, I offer a prayer of gratitude. I thank God for all the blessings in my life, listing many of them individually, and then I ask for guidance on the goal or project I'm working on.

When I meditate I use various methods. But I always think of my main goal before starting. This awareness of my goal before meditating better opens me to intuitive guidance about it.

If you've never meditated before, here's a simple process you can use.

How to Meditate

Find a comfortable place where there are minimal distractions and sit down. You can sit on the floor or in a chair. Avoid lying down because you might fall asleep. It's best to set a timer, an egg timer will do. Many phones also have timer apps you can download. Start with five minutes.

Close your eyes and breathe in and out slowly, focusing on your breath. Think the word *So* on the in-breath and *Hum* on the out-breath. *So Hum* is a mantra—a sound or phrase repeated while meditating—that means *I Am.*

When thoughts come into your mind, simply return to the mantra. When your timer rings, take a moment and sit in silence. Then you're done.

The optimal time for meditating is twenty minutes. I recommend starting with five minutes—if you've never meditated—and adding two to three minutes every week until you're at twenty minutes.

Meditating might feel awkward at first. It might feel like a waste of time. Your mind might give you a dozen or more reason why you could spend the time better doing something else.

Meditate anyway.

There's a Zen saying, "You should sit in meditation for 20 minutes a day. Unless you're too busy, then you should sit for an hour."

Think of it this way. If you're in a jet, you want all the engines working, right? Of course you do! The jet might be able to fly without all the engines, but it's going to be slower, burn more fuel, and be more dangerous because there's less room for error.

Living without daily meditation is like flying in a jet that's missing engines. Why would you?

Maybe a better example is this. Imagine you're a bird. Living without a daily meditation practice is like trying to fly with a strained wing. You might get off the ground but you won't be able to go as far, as high, or as fast as you would if both your wings were healthy. It also might be painful and you could get hurt.

Daily meditation is one of the cornerstones to a fulfilled life. Aside from increasing your ability to receive intuitive guidance, its benefits include clearer thinking, reduced stress, a more peaceful demeanor, increased health, better sleep, increased creativity, better life perspective, and much, much more.

In my experience, daily meditation enhances all the positive traits of my being while reducing my ego's hold on my actions. My life simply flows better when I'm meditating regularly.

Yours will too.

You understand how to open yourself to receiving intuitive guidance. Now it's time to listen.

As stated earlier in this chapter, when you have a feeling, thought, or knowing that you should take an action, *Take It!*

If you're serious about making your dreams and goals reality, you'll act on inspiration. The more you act on your intuition, your inspiration, the more you'll receive and understand intuitive guidance.

Here's a method that helps. Simply set the intention in the morning to understand when you're receiving inspiration and to act on all the inspiration you receive.

To do this, look in the mirror when you're getting ready for your day and say, "I'm open to receiving inspiration. I recognize it when it comes and I act on it." And then do it!

Got it?

Great!

Action Points:
- Inspiration comes in many forms and should never be ignored.
- Trust your inspiration. Take action on it
- The more you heed inspiration, the more you'll receive it
- Daily meditation increases your ability to receive intuitive guidance

Allow Success

"Fear is the only thing that can stop you from living your dreams"
— Paulo Coelho

Understanding the power of the *Law of Action* and using it in your life, knowing your goals, creating an action plan, taking daily action and inspired action, paying attention to feedback... All of these are necessary to living a fulfilled life. They're also critical to effectively reaching your goals. But if you're not allowing success you're seriously hamstringing your results because failing to *allow success* undermines the whole process.

Failing to *allow success* is a form of self-sabotage. It's one of the things your subconscious mind might do to keep your results aligned with your current subconscious beliefs. Remember, your subconscious mind can't stand when reality doesn't fit its beliefs. It will do everything it can to correct the perceived misalignment. That means it's possible for you to do everything right and still sabotage your goals and dreams by not allowing yourself to succeed.

Does that mean you should throw in the towel, give up, or quit working to achieve your goals and dreams? Of course not!

It means you must keep working on your subconscious beliefs—as outlined in the chapter *Your Subconscious Mind*. Once your subconscious beliefs are in harmony with your conscious goals, dreams, and desires you'll see astonishing differences in your life. Then your subconscious mind will do everything in its power to make sure your reality matches its new beliefs.

Here's an example of how this principle changed my life.

Depressed

I was depressed for most of my life, even suicidal for many years. It seemed there was nothing to feel happy about, no joy in my life. Every day was muffled by a dark cloud of sadness.

Then, about 9 years ago as I write this, I experienced an epiphany. *I could choose my thoughts!* And through choosing my thoughts I could change my life. (You can *read* about my transformation in my book: *Break Your Mold.*)

I immediately started using methods like affirmations, subliminal recordings, and goal setting to modify my subconscious beliefs.

Before I knew it, my depression vanished! I'd changed my subconscious beliefs, cast aside the identity of a depressed person, and replaced it with the identity of a resilient, happy person.

With my new subconscious beliefs in place, my subconscious mind was aligned with my conscious desires. It became my ally and started looking for ways to be consistently resilient and happy

I went from a dark, brooding, depressed person to a happy, optimistic, resilient person in only a few months. And, because my subconscious mind is working with me instead of against me, I've stayed there!

That's the power of changing your subconscious beliefs.

What amazing things will you do with your life when your subconscious beliefs and your conscious desires are in harmony?

To test how your subconscious beliefs are aligning with your conscious desires, pay attention to how you feel when you think of your goal. Do you feel excited or anxious, nervous or calm, uncertain or confident?

Feelings of anxiety, nervousness, or uncertainty when thinking of your goal are signs that your subconscious beliefs aren't completely aligned with your conscious desires. Feelings of excitement, calmness, and confidence are signs that your subconscious beliefs are lining up nicely.

How you feel while working on your goal and how easily you start working are indicators of your subconscious beliefs too.

When you set aside time to work on your goal, do you actually do it or do you procrastinate and find reasons to put it off? Procrastination is one of your subconscious mind's greatest weapons when it comes to sabotaging your goals. It's a clear indicator that your subconscious mind isn't completely on your side in this venture.

When your subconscious mind is on your side *you'll feel eager, even excited to work on your goal* because *working on your goal is a privilege*. Working on your goal helps bring your reality closer to your subconscious beliefs. That's what your subconscious mind wants, for reality to match its beliefs.

The best way to overcome procrastination is to notice it and then take the action it's avoiding. Remind yourself that *you want this goal. You want* to *succeed. You want* to *grow*. Avoiding actions that will make your goal reality doesn't make sense. That's like saying you're hungry and then refusing food because eating takes too much effort.

As you create the habit of taking action when you feel like putting something off, you're also retraining your brain to link the two. Meaning; when you feel like procrastinating but choose to take action instead, you create and then strengthen the neural pathway associated with that choice. You're telling your mind that feeling like procrastinating should trigger you to take action. Once that pathway is firmly etched in your mind you'll discover that any time you feel like putting something off, your mind says, "Woah. If we feel like putting this off, then we'd better *do it now!*"

That's powerful! That's getting your subconscious to work for you instead of against you.

When you're working on your goal, how do you feel?

If you feel like you're forcing it or less than excited to work on your goal, then your subconscious beliefs need some fine tuning. Maybe they need a complete overhaul. But if they needed a complete overhaul you probably wouldn't work on your goal. The fact that *you're showing up* and *taking action* means your subconscious beliefs are starting to come around.

Keep using the methods mentioned in the chapter *Your Subconscious Mind* to fine tune your subconscious beliefs. Even when you feel no resistance to working on your goals and dreams it's good to keep reinforcing your new subconscious beliefs. That way old patterns will weaken and eventually get wiped out.

We've discussed the power of our subconscious minds. We understand how to reshape our subconscious beliefs so our subconscious minds work for us. Aside from getting your subconscious beliefs in harmony with your conscious desires, how exactly do you allow success?

The best way I've discovered to allow success is to notice and acknowledge your successes on a regular basis. It's easy to get caught up in whether we're on track for our goal and to focus only on the end result. It's also easy to criticize ourselves if we haven't achieved our goal yet. The problem with these habits are they put you in a constant tension state. This can create anxiety and stress because it leads to feeling like you're always chasing your goal but never succeeding.

Anxiety and stress should never be part of your goal realization process. Even if your goal is a multi-month or multi-year project, you need to feel success on a regular basis. Few of us can maintain the drive necessary to complete a multi-month or multi-year project without feeling successful along the way.

That's part of why it's important to create checkpoints for your goal. Reaching checkpoints gives you positive feedback which reinforces your success.

But what if you miss your checkpoint?

Even missing a checkpoint can reinforce success if you use the information to grow. In writing this book I had an initial checkpoint of having my rough draft finished by Thanksgiving Day 2015. I missed the mark. I was only seventy-five percent done with the first draft by that date.

I could have beaten myself up for not working harder or more on the book. But what would that accomplish?

Right, nothing worthwhile.

Instead I focused on just how much I'd accomplished in the short time I've been writing this book. I decided to write the book—and started the project—less than a month ago, I'm working on it less than two hours a day, and I'm nearly finished! I've been hitting all my daily goals too.

That's something to celebrate!

The fact that I missed my mark for having the rough draft finished tells me that I needed to either dedicate more time each day to writing, revise my daily goals, or revise the length of the book.

I learned a valuable lesson for my next book. That's a good thing too.

So even though I wasn't as far along as I wanted to be on Thanksgiving Day, I still feel successful about the progress I've made!

A good way to recognize your successes is to document them. This tells your subconscious mind that success is desirable. It also helps you look for your successes. Often we fail to recognize our small victories because we're so focused on the end result. This can lead to feeling overwhelmed, like you're never doing enough.

Celebrate all your victories.

Allow yourself to feel good about showing up on the days you didn't feel like it. That's a huge success! How many people let opportunities to work on their goals slip away because they were too tired, they didn't feel up to it, or they got distracted by something else? But *you showed up!*

Allow yourself to feel successful when you move through a sticking point or when you overcome an obstacle on the path of your goal. That means you've grown!

Allow yourself to feel victorious when you realize you need to adjust course—your method or actions—because this knowledge helps you better realize your goal!

It's good to feel success daily. Even on day's you feel like you didn't get much done you can find something to feel successful about. Use the spaces below to celebrate your successes. I've included ten lines.

At the end of the chapter there are also links to either download a .pdf copy of my *Daily Success Log* or purchase your own *Celebration and Success Journal*. That way you can celebrate your successes on a regular basis! (I created the journal for my book *Break Your Mold: The Art of Overcoming Patterns and Behaviors That Hold You Back* and it's perfect for this too.)

My Successes!

1. _____

   _____

2. _____

   _____

3. _____

   _____

4. _____

   _____

5. _____

   _____

6. _____

   _____

7. _____

   _____

8. _____
    _____

9. _____
    _____

10. _____
    _____

As you clear your subconscious mind of disempow-ering beliefs and celebrate your successes more and more, you'll feel less resistance when you work on your goals and dreams. The absence of internal resistance means you've kicked in the afterburner. You're well on your way to realizing your goal.

Keep it up!

Next we'll discuss why your mindset is critical.

Action Points:
- You must allow yourself to succeed
- Working on your goals and dreams is a priv-ilege
- Pay attention to your feelings and thoughts when working on your goals and dreams
- Keep working on your subconscious beliefs
- Celebrate all of your successes

- Download your Daily Success Log .pdf Here: http://bit.ly/DailySuccessLog
- *Purchase* your Celebration and Success Journal Here: http://bit.ly/CelebrateSuccessJournal

Your Mindset

*"If you change the way you look at things, the things
you look at change."*
– Dr. Wayne Dyer

Without the proper mindset it's difficult to achieve your
goals and dreams. And that's an understatement. We've
discussed the importance of working with your subconscious mind to align it with your conscious desires. Now
we'll cover the importance of recognizing and correcting
patterns that interfere with success.

You can be serious about achieving your goals and
dreams. You can work on them every day. You can feel
great about them. But if you have the wrong mindset, or
have patterns of behavior that sabotage you, you'll have
difficulty finishing what you start.

In the past I was serious about success but I had
a fragile mindset. During that time I'd routinely sabotage my success in many areas of my life because I didn't
understand how to overcome behavioral patterns that
hamstrung me. I routinely allowed other influences, real
and imagined, to determine my actions instead of per-
sisting.

Here's an example:

Working Out

I love physical fitness. When I was younger my idea of the ideal body was a bodybuilder's physique. I wanted to be as huge and ripped as possible. Men like Arnold Schwarzenegger, Lee Haney, Tom Platz, Robbie Robinson, & Lou Ferrigno were my idols. I spent hours in the gym, often sacrificing other things so I could workout.

I never had lasting results though. I'd workout for a while, usually six months to a year. I'd make great gains in strength and size. Then something would happen and I'd quit.

I never intended to quit. But each time the cycle repeated, it went like this. I'd miss a few workouts. Then I'd feel guilty about missing the workouts. Then I'd imagine all my friends at the gym were wondering where I'd gone. Then I'd feel ashamed for missing my workouts. Then I'd imagine that my friends were judging me for not showing up and I'd feel more

guilt and shame. Then I'd start label-
ing myself a failure because I'd stopped
working out and I'd panic when I thought
about going to the gym.

During this cycle I'd try to go to the
gym. Often I'd get up, get ready, drive to
the gym, and sit in my car for a while in a
cold sweat. I imagined the silent ridicule
my friends would have for me because I'd
missed some workouts.

My fear of what they thought mixed
with my self-labeling of "being a failure"
was too much for my fragile mindset. I'd
lock up emotionally, like my mind was
stuck in a negative-feedback loop. I'd
sit frozen, physically unable to open the
door, get out of the car, or go into the
gym. In time I'd give in to my panic and
leave.

This scenario played out more times
than I care to count. It started when I
was in high school and continued into my
thirties. I finally learned to overcome this
pattern when I took up skateboarding at
thirty-four. But that's another story.

If you've never experienced this sort of self-induced mental paralysis, being paralyzed from fear "of what others think" might sound silly or strange to you, but it's very real. It's also completely in the mind of the person experiencing it. It becomes their reality because it's where their focus is. This shows how powerful our thoughts are in shaping our personal reality.

The truth is, none of my friends at the gym were close friends. They were acquaintances. They might have recognized that I was missing for the first few workouts, but they wouldn't have tracked whether I showed up or not. They certainly had more important things to worry about. If I'd have come back after missing a few workouts, they most likely would have said, "Hi." And then gone about their business.

No big deal.

All the pressure, guilt, and shame I put on myself was the big deal. My imagination of what they were thinking and how the scenario would play out was the problem. I thought my way into social paralysis.

Our perception of reality becomes our personal reality. My thoughts about what others were thinking and about my personal identity as a failure were my reality.

What I didn't know then, was that I could have changed my thoughts at any time. I could have changed my personal reality at any moment. We all have this power.

I could have thought, "My friends will be glad to see me." Or, "My friends won't care that I've missed a few workouts." Or, "What my friends think about me is no concern of mine. I'm doing what I want." And gone to the gym regardless.

Since I hadn't learned that yet, my pattern continued to wreak havoc on my success with exercising and physical fitness.

Do you have any patterns of behavior that might or perhaps do interfere with your personal success? Can you think of a time when you were doing great and then you did something that derailed the whole process? Has this happened more than once?

If so I recommend grabbing a copy of my book, *Break Your Mold: The Art of Overcoming Patterns and Behaviors That Hold You Back.* It's a comprehensive guidebook that helps you identify and overcome limiting and disempowering behavior.

You can get it here: http://bit.ly/BreakYourMold-Book

Now that we've discussed the importance of a healthy mindset, let's keep moving forward.

Action Points:
- Your mindset is critical to your success
- Recognize and correct patterns that interfere with success

- Thoughts that interfere with your success are a big deal
- Change your thoughts and you change your life

Keep Moving Forward

"Don't only practice your art, but force your way into its secrets, for it and knowledge can raise men to the divine."
— *Beethoven*

Once you start experiencing success, you must keep moving forward! Complacency can follow minor success. Avoid this trap. It's another way your subconscious mind tries to keep you stuck. You might have thoughts like, "I got so much done yesterday. I deserve a break." Or, "Look at how far I've come, I can take it easy this week."

When you have thoughts similar to these, simply say, "Thank you for your input." And then *take action anyway!* It's imperative you remind your subconscious mind that *your goal is important*. Remember the reasons *your goal is important* to you, *get excited* about it, and then *take action anyway!*

Understand, there's no such thing as coasting on the path to success. When you coast, you're actually losing momentum. Lose enough momentum and you're standing still. You'll never achieve your goals and dreams if you start coasting. Period.

Harsh? Maybe...

True? Definitely!

You want the truth! You're reading this book because you want to know the secrets of using the *Law of Action* in your life. One of the biggest secrets is this: *You must use it!* Knowing about the *Law of Action* and failing to use it is like asking for your dream but refusing to hold out your hand, to take it, when it's offered to you!

It makes no sense.

But people do it all the time. They ask for knowledge that will change their lives, they get the information, and then never take action on it. Those people are in love with the idea of achieving their goals but unwilling to do the work. They're happy holding onto a dream without trying to make it reality.

Are you one of those people?

Or are you one of the few who goes the extra step and implements the new knowledge in their lives?

Right, *You Take Action!*

You use your new knowledge. You practice it and work with it until it becomes second nature. That's why you're reading this book. You're serious about success!

You've got to adopt the mentality of a rhino when it comes to working on your goals and dreams. Keep your head high, your shoulders squared, and plow forward. Resistance shows up in your path; plow through it. Obstacles show up in your path; plow through them or go around them. You're tired, you're overwhelmed, you're sad, or you're any other of the many emotional or physical states that can interfere with your success; plow your way forward.

What I'm saying is that there is always a way to move ahead, there is always a way to make progress. It's up to you to find the way, get help with it, and learn your way through or around it. It's up to you to keep taking action.

When *you do this*, when *you take consistent action* on your goals and dreams, when you keep moving forward no matter what, you'll *discover success* you never imagined.

Action Points:
- Take Consistent Action
- Use your new knowledge until it becomes second nature
- Adopt the mentality of a rhino when it comes to achieving your goals and dreams
- There is always a way to keep moving forward

Now *is* The Time

"You can't just sit there and wait for people to give you that golden dream; you've got to get out there and make it happen for yourself."
– Diana Ross

Now is always the best time to take action. Procrastination is the biggest success killer out there. Thinking, "I'll do it tomorrow." Or, "I'll do it later." Really means, "It's not important enough to do now."

Consider this:

When do we want success?
Now!
When do we want to work on creating it?
Tomorrow!
Wrong answer.

When you're using the *Law of Action* to achieve your goals and dreams, you'll receive inspiration. When you receive inspiration *you must act on it!*

Yes, there are times when it's not feasible to drop everything you're doing and take the inspired action. But you can always write it down. You can create a calendar appointment to work on your inspiration at the soonest available opportunity. You can record a reminder in your phone.

The point is, you can and must take action on your inspiration when you have it. That tells your subconscious mind, God, and the Universe that you want inspiration. It also shows that you're serious about your success.

And *You are Serious About Your Success!*

"Now is the time to take action!" Also means you must assess how you manage your time. Are you using your available time wisely or are you wasting it?

Only you know the answer to that question. As you know, it's possible to have the appearance of working on your goals and dreams without actually working on them.

The truth is, you have this moment. The past is a memory and the future is a dream, unwritten. This moment is your truth, your power, your fires of creation.

How are you using it?

Are you *doing what you love?*

Are you *serving others?*

Are you *making the world a better place?*

If not, why not?

You have the power of The *Law of Action* at your fingertips.

You have the ability to do anything you desire with your life.

You are a perfect creation, imbued with miraculous power!

Now is the time to use it!

Love,
Roland

http://www.RolandByrd.co/

If *you enjoyed this book*, please leave a review online and tell your friends!

Thank you.

Roland

Ready to *Change Your Life*?

Enroll in Life 180 University *Today* and *Discover*:

- Exactly how to identify and change problem areas in your life.
- How to use your subconscious mind to help you change.
- How to create a life-long habit of excellence.
- How to discover and become the best you.
- And best of all, how to make these changes last!

http://www.180-u.com

More Books By Roland Byrd:

Your Blueprint, Life by Design
The Pi of Life
Reflections
A Slice of Madness
Break Your Mold
Break Your Mold The Workbook
Break Your Mold Celebration and Success Journal
Another Slice of Pi
*The Prosperity Factor with Joe Vitale

Available From:

http://www.rolandbyrd.co/books-by-roland-byrd/
http://amazon.com/author/rolandbyrd

*Roland is a contributing author to this book

Hire Roland to Speak for Your Organization or at Your Event:

http://www.rolandbyrd.co/roland-speaks/

Roland Byrd is the author of seven personal development and transformational books, contributing author to the bestselling book *The Prosperity Factor*—with Joe Vitale, and the founder of *Life 180 University*. His passion is helping people unlock their true power, be their best selves, and master their destiny.

You Want Roland at Your Event!

Roland presents with passion, humor, and energy. He engages his audience and is easy to understand. He uses analogies, stories from his own life, and real-world examples to drive home the principles he teaches.

Book Roland for Your Event Today!
http://www.rolandbyrd.co/roland-speaks/